Child Custody and Visitation: A Christian Perspective

By: Robert W. Rushing, Jr.

Wilberforce Press, Inc.

2013

We live in an increasingly secular world.   This is an inescapable fact. We also live in an age in which it is almost impossible to escape the constant barrage of material through the media intended to manipulate the beliefs and the faith of your family. Sadly, this manipulation is invariably of a sort calculated to marginalize the institution of marriage, destabilize the family, and corrupt your children.

It is no accident that the past forty years have seen the divorce rate skyrocket in America. This was the inevitable result of no fault divorce laws, which turned the dissolution of a marriage from a last option into a common, mundane experience hardly worth mentioning after the fact. Multiple marriages and divorces are common, and many people are no more hesitant to end a marriage than they would be to change socks. The sanctity of the institution of marriage has been, possibly irretrievably, broken. Unfortunately, the Christian church has not been immune to the effect of all of this.

Thus, it is increasingly more difficult to achieve a successful marriage, and by extension, family life. Far too many church goers offer lip service to traditional values, but in practice, prefer the convenience of the modern approach. As a result, their instinct at the first sign of trouble is to go to the phone book or the internet, and pick a lawyer.

From there, it only gets worse. If there are children to raise, particularly young children, it will be a priority for the Christian parent to raise his or her child in his faith. The possibility of being deprived of the right to do so is deeply disturbing, and very real. The current state of the law provides no consideration in custody cases to the religious beliefs or values of a parent, instead imposing its own secular set of values which have evolved from a standard of "best interest of the child." It goes without saying that those beliefs and values are increasingly alien to what were seen as consensus family values only a few years before.

Thus, when a marriage goes on the rocks, the Christian father or mother is faced with multiple problems. First of all, he is faced with a legal system that had made the process of dissolving a marriage quick, relatively painless, and user friendly. Worse, once he is forced into these hostile waters, he is required to navigate a system that is at best indifferent to his belief system, and at worst, hostile.

The fight is uphill, and the stakes are tremendous. Depending on the beliefs and sincerity of his spouse, there is the issue of whether, and to what extent, his child will be raised on the teachings of Jesus Christ. There is the prospect of an uphill battle to remain a positive influence and role model for the children, in a society which tends to marginalize men and especially fathers. Last but not least, there is the need to handle what might very well be a contentious, difficult, high stakes battle with his former spouse, and yet to do so in a way consistent with Christian ethics and the teachings of Christ.

None of this is easy. Many of the choices to be made are distinguished in shades of grey. What might seem the right course in the heat of a moment may lead to many sleepless nights down the road. Too often, the issue is whether the short and long term trauma of a contested custody case is worthwhile for a child, if the end result is a better home life. Such questions can only be answered by those that know the child and the family best, not by attorneys, guardians, or judges. Unfortunately, those are the individuals who are left to make the call.

This book is not about the options available to help you save your marriage. There are many excellent sources for such information, and consequentially, no need to address that topic here. Suffice to say that you owe it to yourself, your spouse, and especially your children to do everything reasonably possible to save your marriage and your family.

In my practice, I have discovered a funny thing about marriages on the rocks. More often than not, the problem which is threatening to cause a breakdown of the relationship and ultimately divorce is actually more difficult to solve when and if the two parties split.

For example, I once had a consultation with a young married couple who appeared to be fighting almost exclusively over bills. The credit card was had been overused to the point that it was still warm to the touch. Then one of them lost a job, which divided their income in half. They were facing foreclosure and repossession of their home. Creditors were calling at all hours.

In these kinds of circumstances, almost any couple would begin to argue. Yet, talking with them, it was apparent that the source of the friction between them was their fear about their economic circumstances, and nothing else. Something else was equally clear. The wife was pregnant and their second child was due in a few weeks.

I began by reminding them of something that should be obvious, but which practically everyone seems to forget. As bad as the financial situation was, breaking up was only going to make the problems exponentially worse. After all, there is nothing to the plan of having one party move out, purchase a second set of essential possessions such as appliances, furniture, television, etc., and ultimately, hire a divorce lawyer or two that was going to improve the bottom line.

I suggested that, before I was paid anything past the initial consultation fee, they fill out the financial disclosure forms the court requires in a contested divorce case. Looking at the income sources, and the itemized debts, it would then be possible to make a plan to deal with the problem. It turned out that much of the problem was unsecured credit card debt.

This meant that those debts could be dealt with effectively through a bankruptcy. While this is an option that involves ethical concerns we will address later in the book, it is also a fact of which the issuing banks are well aware. I suggested a reduced monthly payment figure that would allow them to maintain essentials such as the mortgage, car payment and utilities, and suggested that they offer this figure in compromise.

After some back and forth, the credit card company agreed to the short term modification. This allowed some breathing time, during which the wife had her child and was able to return to the workforce. With the stress level down appreciably, the arguments became much less frequent. The marriage was continued and the family remained intact. While it was not one of my more profitable cases, it was one of the more satisfying.

Of course, the same can be said for the relative difficulty of raising children. It is easier for two good parents to feed, care for, clothe, educate, and instill values in a child, although, as anyone who has ever attempted it will tell you, it is still no cake walk. Doing it alone is nearly impossible. Again, there are good reasons to think twice about breaking up such a partnership.

For the same reasons, it must be a priority to save whatever part of such a partnership can be saved. Whatever the reason for the breakdown of the marriage, and however just the reason for your anger and resentment may be, it is essential to get along with parent of your child as well as possible. This is necessary first for the child, secondly because it is consistent with all Christian teaching which speak to the subject, and finally, by reason of your own self- interest. (By which I mean that, long after the war for the children has ended, you will still have to deal with each other. The other parent is not going away, unless you can prove in a court of law that he or she is unfit. Besides, a motivated babysitter who will work for free and whom the kids love is a wonderful thing.)

This book is divided into three parts. The first will address scripture that speaks to the relationship between husband and wife, and parent and child. The second will inform you as to what to expect in a divorce action with a contested custody issue, where your faith is an issue for yourself, the opposing party, or the court. The final will discuss tactics. A Christian might find him or herself constrained by his values in this situation, but should nevertheless be able to fight aggressively to protect his children, and to a lesser extent his financial well-being.

CHAPTER ONE

THE GOOD SAMARITAN

Jesus told the story of the Good Samaritan to answer a man's question of who someone's neighbor might be. "A man was going down from Jerusalem to Jericho, and fell into the hands of robbers, who stripped him, beat him, and went away, leaving him half dead. Now by chance a priest was going down that road, and when he saw him, he passed to the other side. So likewise a Levite, when he came to the place and saw him, passed by on the other side. But a Samaritan while traveling came near him, and when he saw him, was moved with pity.

He went to him and bandaged his wounds, having poured oil and wine on them. Then he put him on his own animal, brought him to an inn, and took care of him. The next day he took out two denarii, gave them to the innkeeper, and said "Take care of him and when I come back, I will repay you whatever more you spend." Which of these three do you think, was a neighbor to the man who fell into the hands of the robbers? He said "The one who showed him mercy." Jesus said to him, "Go and do likewise." Luke 10:30-37.

This story does not speak directly to the issues which result from marital dissolution and the separation of a family. Nevertheless, it is a powerful and directly applicable message. It instructs Christians, however and whenever possible, to protect, care for, and heal others who are in physical or psychological pain. The Samaritan, of course, extends his kindness to a stranger. Can there be any doubt that, had the parable been about a wife, a child, or a family member, the message would have been the same?

The point is re-emphasized in the story of the Prodigal Son. Jesus said, "There was a man who had two sons. The younger of them said to his father, "Father give me the share of the property that will belong to me." So he divided the property between them. A few days later the young son gathered all that he had and traveled to a distant country, and there he squandered his property in dissolute living.

When he had spent everything, a severe famine took place throughout that country, and he began to be in need. So he went and hired himself out to one of the citizens of that country, who sent him to the field to feed the pigs. He would gladly have filled himself with the pods that the pigs were eating, and no one gave him anything. But when he came to himself he said, "How many of my father's hired hands have bread enough to spare, but here I am dying of hunger!" I will get up and go to my father and I will say to him, "Father, I have sinned against heaven and before you. I am no longer worthy to be called your son. Treat me like one of your hired hands."

So he set off and went to his father. But while he was still far off, his father saw him and was filled with compassion; he ran and put his arms around him and kissed him. Then the son said to him, "Father, I have sinned against heaven and before you; I am no longer worthy to be called your son. But the father said to his slaves, "Quickly, bring out a robe-the best one-and put it on him; put a ring on his finger and sandals on his feet. And get the fatted calf and kill it, and let us eat and celebrate, for this son of mine was dead and is alive again, he was lost and is found." And they began to celebrate. Luke 15:11-24.

There is a consensus that the parable is a metaphor for the infinite love and patience of the Almighty for his highly imperfect flock. While that is no doubt true, that does not mean that the story is not instructive when taken literally. It is suggestive of how Christ would teach us to treat our husbands, wives, and children when their behavior disappoints or injures us.

More directly, the Bible tells us to "Take pleasure in the wife of your youth." (Proverbs 5:18) At a time centuries before the concept of divorce was introduced into Christian life, the point is directly addressed. In reflection, that fact is extraordinary and fascinating.

Of course, nobody said it would be easy. Nearly fifty percent (50%) of the marriages in this county end in divorce. Even this sad statistic does not fully express the extent of the problem. While there is no study to support my observation, I have seen a clear trend over the years. Increasingly with time, couples enter into marriage with the expectation that the relationship is only temporary, and consequentially prepare for its dissolution from the beginning.

A great deal more is expected of the Christian. He or she is expected to show the kindness of the Samaritan, even for a stranger on the highway. He or she is likewise instructed to exercise the patience and unconditional love of the father of the Prodigal son, even in the worst circumstances.

This book, of course, is not about reconciliation. However, it would be wrong to proceed without making the point that marriage is a far more sacred institution than our society currently gives it credit for. You owe it to yourself, your spouse, and your family to do whatever is reasonably possible to save your marriage.

However, the reality is that you may well have no alternative but to make the tactical decisions involved in a contested divorce. When this occurs, the repercussions will irreparably change the lives of both husband and wife, and very often, the lives of a great many others as well.

The decisions will be made by a system which can appear at best slow and arbitrary; at worst, hostile. If you are reading this book, you are well aware that the animosity towards Christians and Christian values is at a toxic level in our society. The courts are no exception, and sadly, are arguably the place where such attitudes initially took seed and flourished.

This is not to say that all, or even most, family court judges and officials are biased against Christians. However, anyone who has spent substantial time in the court system over the past two decades, if honest, will acknowledge the change. Once in the not too distant past, traditional family values, church membership, and profession of faith were prerequisites. The testimony of a minister was considered unimpeachable. Today, such considerations have been marginalized in child custody cases.

Faced with these new and alien rules, there is a tendency to ask the question of whether a Christian should submit to the authority of the court at all. The thought of fleeing a jurisdiction, or talking other extra legal action, comes to mind. These alternatives are counterproductive in the long run, and I believe, against the teachings of Christ.

In his book "The Cross and Christian Ministry' Don Carson defines what he refers to as "a world Christian." He identifies this as a useful model for addressing the new and diverse challenges that are faced by the Christian in the complex modern world. The term means four things:

1. Their allegiance to Jesus Christ and his kingdom is self consciously set above all national, cultural, linguistic, and racial allegiances.

2. Their commitment to the church, Jesus' messianic community, is to the church everywhere, wherever the church is truly manifest, and not only to its manifestation on home turf.

3. They see themselves first and foremost as citizens of the heavenly kingdom and therefore consider all other citizenship as a secondary matter.

4. As a result, they are single minded and sacrificial when it comes to the paramount mandate to evangelize and make disciples. (Carson, "The Cross and the Ministry" 117).

Thus, the question must be addressed by reference to scripture. Despite the changes in our culture, we are fortunate to live in a nation still relatively tolerant of Christianity and Christian values. The early Christians, by contrast, were subjects of ancient Rome, which frequently put church members to death. Their documented thoughts on the relationship of the Christian with his government cannot be fully appreciated without considering the context.

The Apostle Paul wrote the following in a letter to the Romans:

"Everyone must submit to the governing authorities, for there is no authority except from God, and those that exist are instituted by God. So then, the one who resists the authority is opposing God's command, and those who oppose it will bring judgment on themselves (Romans 13:1-2 HCSB)."

"For rulers are not a terror to good conduct, but to bad. Do you want to be unafraid of the authority? Do good and you will have its approval. For government is God's servant to you for good. But if you do wrong, be afraid, because it does not carry the sword for no reason. For government is God's servant, an avenger that brings wrath on the one who does wrong." (13:3-4).

This seems a good place to start. As a Christian, it is right that you comply with the law. You should pay your taxes, register for the draft, and obey the laws of the highway, because it is consistent with the teachings of Jesus to do so. However, I personally do not believe that these passages constitute a complete answer.

To believe otherwise would be a highly selective view of the relevant Bible passages. The best example to my mind being the words of Peter and the apostles in the book of Acts 5:27-29.

And when they had brought them, they set them before the council, and the high priest asked them,

Saying, Did not we straitly command you that ye should not teach in this name? and behold,

Ye have filled Jerusalem with your doctrine, and intent to bring this man's blood upon us.

Then Peter and the other apostles answered and said, We ought to obey God rather than men.

(KJV)

The apostles were not alone in making this choice. Throughout history, men of conscious have risk life, limb, and property to challenge injustice. Often, as in the case of our founding fathers, this has involved a challenge to an entire system of government. More often, it has simply meant a commitment to work within a system for effective change.

This could mean advocating political reform in your state as to what laws are on the books, or how judges are selected. These are certainly battleground areas in the social wars, and the failure of the Christian community to have its voice heard has been at great costs. More often, it simply means that you must commit to the expenditure of spiritual and financial resources necessary to win your case.

We are engaged in a societal war for the right to raise our children as we wish. Usually, the battles are small ones between parents with conflicting beliefs and values. Invariably, however, federal and state government is a player. Much as its agents and servants might argue otherwise, it is anything but impartial or disinterested.

There is a fine balance between the obligation to respect state authority and the right to challenge social injustice. The answers might best be found in careful reflection and prayer. Be aware that you are not alone.

If I take the wings of the morning,

And dwell in the uttermost parts of the sea;

Even there shall thy hand lead me,

And thy right hand hold me.

If I say, Surely the darkness shall cover me;

Even the night shall be light about me.

Yea, the darkness hideth not from thee;

But the night shineth as the day.

(Psalms 139)

CHAPTER TWO

THE PLAYERS AND THEIR ROLES

If you are involved in a contested custody case, it is first necessary to know the players. Only with a complete understanding of their roles, is it possible to make intelligent choices in how to deal with them.

In a contested case, it is almost a certainty that both parties will have an attorney. When asked, most people express confidence that they know what an attorney does. However, I usually find that they are not clear on the finer points, and this can lead to trouble.

An attorney is an advocate. Within certain ethical constraints (more on that later), his or her job is to get the client what they want; nothing wrong with that. The problem is that few people truly understand the extent of that obligation.

It is not in his or her job description to arbitrate between right and wrong, or to advance the interest of any third party. The attorney is held to a duty of strict confidentiality as to anything his client has told him about a case, to the extent that wrongful disclosure of information can result in the loss of his license. He is not in a position, whatever his personal values or beliefs, to advance the interest of even the most sympathetic adverse party. He is under a duty of enforced institutional bias.

In other words, he or she is a hired gun for the other side. The best you can hope for in a lawyer representing an adverse party is a candid admission of this. I do not recommend meeting with an attorney without a lawyer of your own in such situations. However, if you do so, expect a detailed explanation of his or her ethical obligations, and usually, a written disclosure form to be provided before you speak with him or her. If this does not occur, consider it a red flag and be skeptical of everything that follows.

In other words, NEVER trust a lawyer who is representing a party with interests adverse to you. This means that you should never do the following things:

1. NEVER sign documents in his or her office without an adequate opportunity to review them.

This would almost invariably mean taking them out of his or her office, usually for a consultation with some other unbiased professional who can interpret them for you. If he or she refused to allow you to leave with the documents, something is wrong. Do not sign.

Likewise, if he or she offers to interpret them for you, listen but be skeptical. It is entirely possible that you will be given answers which are truthful, but still misleading. The drafting of settlement agreements and court orders is an art, complex and difficult to penetrate for those who do not practice in the field. A simple twist of a phrase can have tremendous effect down the road.

Finally, if you are given a short, arbitrary deadline to sign the documents or face some sort of consequences, be even more skeptical. To be clear, the phrase "arbitrary deadline" does not include the situation in which settlement is being negotiated on the courthouse steps. However, if there is no obvious reason for a high pressure sales tactic, adopt the same rationale you might employ in a used car lot. Turn and walk away.

2. NEVER discuss the facts of your case with him or her. It is entirely possible that this person will one day ask you questions on the witness stand, with the purpose of discrediting you or your testimony. When you give him or her facts and details about your life, your marriage, or your relationship with your children, this is only gist for the mill.

3. NEVER agree to pay a portion of his or her fee without the advice of counsel. The less scrupulous in our profession love to browbeat naïve litigants into paying fees that would never be awarded in trial. The rationale is that the services they are providing are benefitting both parties. While this might be at least partially true, it does not change the fact that the lawyer is a hired gun in the employ of somebody else.

The second significant figure in a custody action is the Guardian ad Litem. This is an easily translated Latin phrase which means "Guardian in Law." This person is either chosen by the parties, or selected by the judge. Their role is to independently investigate the situation surrounding the custody issue, and make a report to the court.

Technically, the Guardian has no real decision making authority. The reality, however, is far different. There is usually a close working relationship between the two, with the Judge seeing the Guardian as his or her eyes outside of the courtroom. Too often, the Guardian is credited as being a benevolent, unbiased observer, who is the best authority on all issues affecting the child. Consequentially, the litigant is often faced with the same uphill struggle as a small town defendant in traffic court.

The Guardian will interview you, the other parent, and depending on age, possibly the child as well. Depending on her preference, you may be interviewed in her office, at your home during a scheduled time, or possibly an unannounced home visit. The guardian, as a matter of course, will visit the other parent. Depending on the situation, she might also interview school teachers, social workers, health care providers, and other significant individuals in the life of your child.

The Guardian will do something else early on in the case as well. You will receive a letter requesting that you pay a substantial amount of money for his or her services upfront, in a relatively short period of time. From there, you and the other party to the case will be on the clock. In other words, you will receive hourly billings for the work performed by the guardian, which can often exceed the cost of your own lawyer.

Since the Guardian does not represent you, he or she is not bound by the ethical constraints imposed on the relationship you have with your lawyer. Since he or she is purportedly unbiased, the report he presents to the judge has incalculable effect on the attitude of the judge towards both parties.

Possibly most importantly of all, the Guardian is most likely the only individual who will actually ask your child where he or she prefers to live. In most states, it is at least theoretically possible for the Judge to interview the child in chambers. However, the most Judges are unwilling to do so, and leave this chore to the Guardian.

In other words, this is a person you cannot afford to alienate. He has tremendous influence over the outcome of your case, operates with little or no accountability, and is enabled to charge and collect fees which are often arbitrary and excessive. Much like a policeman, the Guardian is in a position to do much good or much harm quickly and irrevocably. Getting a good one is crucial.

This is why the choice of a Guardian is such a crucial step in the litigation process. Typically, the attorneys or the parties casually pick a name from a short list of qualified attorneys who regularly accept such appointments. The fact that what is going on is essentially the appointment of an adjunct judge, who will whisper in the ear of the presiding judge throughout the trial, is lost on most clients.

The Guardian is only slightly less important than the presiding judge.

The presiding Judge, at least at the trial level, makes all the decisions in the case. It is he or she that evaluates the credibility of testimony and the validity of legal arguments. While he may be accountable for erroneous or unfair decisions at some future date, the odds of this are slim.

Few cases are ever appealed to a higher court, due mostly to prohibitive costs. Of the few litigants who do appeal, only a small number succeed. Generally, family court judges are well aware of the kind of mistakes that can make an Order subject to reversal, and avoid them. Likewise, appellate judges tend to give the benefit of the doubt to their peers in the lower courts, absent some compelling reason to do otherwise.

CHAPTER THREE

DETECTING BIAS

In many ways, our country still tends to follow Europe. As such, a recent, lightly reported news story from the United Kingdom might be a sign of the times. It reports an unprecedented action by a high church official of the Church of England, specifically, the former Archbishop of Canterbury.

"Lord Carey, the former Archbishop of Canterbury and other church leaders will urge the Master of the Rolls and other senior judges to stand down from future Court of Appeals hearings involving cases of religious discrimination because of the judges' perceived bias against Christianity. Senior churchmen do not think Christians have any chance of a fair ruling if the latest significant hearing is heard in front of those judges who, they argue, have already shown a lack of understanding of Christian beliefs." (Daily Mail 7/26/13).

One does not have to look too far to see the winds of change here at home. They are essentially unavoidable. We are reminded of them every time we hear the phrase "holiday season" substituted for the word "Christmas," lament the passing of school prayer, or simply turn on TV. While it is debatable when it began, there is no arguing that a sustained and powerful effort to marginalize and ultimately eliminate the Christian faith from American is underway.

For the moment, however, the question is this. Are the principle players in your child custody case playing for the other side?   If so, the results could be disastrous for you and your family. You owe it to yourself to find out as much as possible about these individuals BEFORE they are empowered to take your life into their hands.

The exception here is the attorney for the other parent. He or she, by definition, is duty bound to assist his client to the furthest extent possible. Any motivation other than the simple fact of an attorney client relationship is irrelevant.

The situation is much different relative to the Guardian ad Litem. This individual is usually chosen by the parties through a consent order, or at least, by their lawyers. The situation is a lot like buying something at a store. Until you make a selection, all of the power is with you. After you make a purchase, the power goes over to the newly appointed Guardian.

This means that there must be a great deal of care in the selection process. Most likely, at some point in your time as a parent, you have chosen a baby sitter. When the need arose, it is safe to assume that you didn't just go out into the street and announce that you would be willing to pay someone to watch your child for a few hours.

Most likely, the process was more like this. Unless you already knew someone who could do the job, and were familiar with that person's reputation, you asked around. You probably gave careful thought to even the question of who might be a proper person to recommend a babysitter.

When a name was mentioned, you asked follow up questions. Only after an informal screening process did you actually call the person and interview them. You might have even done a computer search of the babysitter's name, just to be sure that there was nothing to worry about.

Why, then, would you not do the same as to the appointment of a Guardian Ad Litem? This person, after all, will have tremendous influence over the question of where and how your child is raised to adulthood, and help define your role in the process. His or her actions might well be more important to determining what kind of person your child becomes than anyone save the parents themselves.

Too often, a Christian forced into custody litigation makes a mistaken assumption that can have tragic consequences. He or she assumes that, because the individual in question is a practicing lawyer and apparently qualified to serve as a guardian, that this means the individual will be objective and unbiased. In truth, the pool of potential Guardians in your area will represent a wide range of opinions, values and attitudes, with which you may or may not be comfortable. This applies as to the question of what they consider to be good parenting, and equally as much as to the question of what they consider to be ethical obligation to the court.

In other words, you need to be proactive as to finding a Guardian who is at least respectful of your values and your faith. If you fail to do so, it could make the next several months of your life much more difficult, or at worse, cost you the right to raise your child. Here are some basic rules with regards to the process of selecting a guardian.

First of all, if you are representing yourself, follow this simple rule. NEVER agree to the choice of Guardian proposed by the other side, unless you are extremely familiar with the person. As we have already discussed, the attorney who represents the opposing party has a job to do, and that job is not to advance your best interests. He or she is also aware of the power that the Guardian has in the process, and naturally wants to choose an individual who would be sympathetic to the interests o f his client.

Instead, do some legwork at this point. First, find out the names of several individuals who regularly act as Guardians in the jurisdiction. In many places, the Clerk of Court maintains a list of those who are qualified to serve and regularly appointed.

If possible, get a copy of the list. If this is not possible, simply go to the internet or the local phone directors, and look under "Attorneys" and then "Family Court." You will find that many of those attorneys indicate through their ads that they are available to accept such appointments. If this is not possible, simply ask around with those who are in a position to know about such things. This can extend to attorney friends, and of course, anyone you know who been involved in child custody litigation in his or her recent past.

Once you have a list of names, research those people. You can start with a simple search of the attorney name on "Google", "Bing", or some other search engine. This should take you to the web site for the attorney or his or her firm. Once you have located this, note the following things:

1. Does the web site indicate anything about the values and priorities of the firm? For example, is the attorney involved in a cooperative relationship with a state social services agency? Does he or she indicate membership in any organizations? What do these relationships say about him or her? Is he or she a church member? Is family court litigation his or her sole area of practice, or is it one of several priorities? Finally, what can you expect as far as hourly billing expenses from this attorney or firm? If he or she has a blog, carefully read everything that has been posted.

The website, of course, is essentially an advertising brochure. While you can learn a great deal here, it will not tell you everything. To get a fuller picture, you should also look for the following:

2. Check the state bar website. Here, in most states, you can find out if the attorney in question has been disciplined by the state bar, and if so, why. You might also be able to find out what state bar committees the attorney is involved in, which can shed some light on his or her priorities.

3. If your search reveals cases in which the attorney has been involved, review them. It is worth noting what positions the attorney has argued in previous matters. However, you should keep in mind that just because an attorney has argued a legal or moral position in court, this does not mean that this is his or her own personal belief. There are many reasons why an attorney is often forced to advocate for clients and ideas that he might not agree with. Of course, a consistent pattern of taken a certain position in litigation is indicative of choices on his or her part, and therefore telling.

4. In the spirit that turnabout is fair play check the attorney out on social media sites. This is the most likely place to find candid and unguarded commentary. Always check out the name of the attorney, and if he or she is married, his or her spouse, on such sites as Facebook, Linked, and Pintarest. It might also be worthwhile to do a quick check on family members and friends, if this information is available.

5. Finally, just ask around. If you know people in your church who have been in the situation, ask them about the Guardian (and the Judge, more on that later.) However, always take the information they provide with a grain of salt. Remember that their observations will of necessity be colored by their feelings towards what would have been a very emotional process, and that few people are able to be objective about their own conduct. Still, and again, if you find the same thing being said over and over, there is nothing more persuasive than a trend.

6. ALWAYS find out if the potential Guardian has any past working relationship with the opposing attorney or your adverse party. If so, find out everything you can about this past working relationship, especially how often the two have collaborated. Be very skeptical of allowing this person to be appointed in your case.

Once you have gone through this process, Try to come up with a list of three to five potential Guardians with whom you might be comfortable. If you are negotiating with the adverse party to select one, do not suggest your first choice initially. Chances are that your first suggestion will be vetoed for the same reasons we discussed earlier. DO NOT, however, propose the appointment of anyone with whom you are not completely comfortable.

If you are unable to agree to the appointment of a guardian, the court will appoint one for you. This can often be a reasonable alternative to working with an adverse party to find a mutually acceptable person. Keep in mind that, if you have financial concerns relative to the costs of the Guardian, the court might consider this in its choice if the issue is raised with the court. There can be tremendous differences in the hourly billing costs and retainer fees, even among attorneys in the same jurisdiction.

The same considerations apply as to the presiding judge. The only difference is the fact that your choices are far more limited. Usually, you would investigate the background of the presiding judge for the purpose of knowing how to persuade your audience, as opposed to selecting it.

It is worth noting that, as opposed to the potential Guardian, the name of the judge is far more likely to reveal published articles or opinions in a search. Also unlike the Guardian, the judge is under no duty to advocate a position he or she finds distasteful. Therefore, what she writes in a court order can pretty much be taken to the bank as representative of his or her belief system and values. You can plan accordingly.

For example, I once tried a custody case in which my client was a reformed alcoholic, who had been in several alcohol related accidents. We discovered that the presiding judge had lost a child due to the actions of a drunk driver. Not surprisingly, he had the reputation of having very little tolerance for anyone who abused alcohol. This made the issue of my client's past conduct even more front and center. I spent far more time addressing his sobriety; even bringing in counselors and physicians. It was crucial to our favorable result in the case.

However, if you find that you are facing a trial judge with clear and expressed bias towards those of the Christian faith, you do have options. They include:

A. You can ask the judge to remove him or herself from the case. This can be done by formal motion which is referred to in the laws as a motion to recuse. It cannot be emphasized enough that the filing of this motion is a two edged sword, as likely to hurt one litigant as the other.

The problem is that, in order for the motion to succeed, you must argue that the judge is biased, and cannot make an unprejudiced ruling in the case. Since the motion must be argued before the very judge who is the subject of the motion, you are essentially insulting the judge prior to trial. If he or she takes offense, there is nothing to stop him from denying your motion, and then making life extremely hard for you at trial.

For this reason, I do not believe that a motion to recuse should be filed without the assistance of an attorney.

B. In most jurisdictions, there are several possible trial judges for any one case. If there is one in particular who needs to be avoided, the best approach is to be actively involved in the scheduling process.

The court system calls this "forum shopping," and frowns on it. For this reason, you do not want to candidly admit that you want to avoid a particular judge, or have the case heard before a particular judge. Instead, take this approach:

Go the court web site, or call the local clerk of court, and get a calendar for the terms of court in which your case might be scheduled. The schedule will ordinarily show what or which judges are presiding at each particular time. From there, it may be a relatively simple matter to schedule around a judge you wish to avoid, or towards one you want to appear before. Lawyers do this all of the time.

Keep in mind, however, that this is not an infallible strategy. Judges often substitute for one another, or change schedules. In most places, you will not be advised of any change until shortly before trial. Many times, I have had a surprised switch in the court schedule, and argued a case very differently as a result.

C. In the worst cases, you might consider whether to relocate. This is admittedly a high risk strategy. Before even discussing the idea, it should be emphasized that IF YOU HAVE BEEN SERVED WITH PAPERS IN A JURISDICITION, IT IS UNLIKELY THAT YOU CAN LEAVE THE AREA AND PREVENT THE LOCAL COURT FROM HEARING THE CASE. Further, if you fail to appear at a scheduled hearing after receiving notice, the court will almost certainly rule in favor of the adverse party on all issues, making your case an uphill battle from that point on.

This strategy works best when the distance involved is either very short or very long. If the change is simply the crossing of a county or parish line, the courts are not as likely to frown on your conduct. This is because the effect on the life of the child is minimized. He or she is not being permanently deprived of his parent, his school, or his friends. Also, there is no perceived design to prevent the state from exercising its interest in protecting a citizen of the state; an interest that has been given increasingly more emphasis over time.

The result of relocation over a county line might be a venue argument among lawyers. Without going into great detail as to the law in this area, it is generally true that the issue of how long you have lived at the new address will be central to where the case is tried. In other words, if you are inclined to make this kind of a move, the sooner you do it the better.

If the move is over a long distance, such as to another state or country, the venue argument might essentially decide the entire custody battle. The judge of the state from which the child has been removed will view the act of relocation with hostility, and be highly receptive to the protests of the parent who has remained in state. This will be particularly true where the effect of the relocation has been to cut off visitation or contact between the child and one parent.

Likewise, the sheer expense of litigating in a distance forum might force the hand of one or the other parent. In a worst case scenario, there may be competing child custody cases ongoing in two jurisdictions, with two teams of lawyers for each parent. This can result in a catastrophic money drain that few can afford.

Again, this is a choice not to be taken lightly. I would recommend that such a decision not be made without the benefit of legal advice. Most states operate under a version of a model law known as the "Uniform Child Custody Jurisdiction Act" which is intended to prevent parents from taking a child out of her home state, relocating, and quickly filing for an emergency custody order. The language of the statute is somewhat fact specific, and prescribes minimum periods of time in which a child must be in a state before its courts have jurisdiction.

There is finally what I refer to as the "nuclear option," filing an ethics complaint against the judge. This is the bad idea for multiple reasons, with the near certainty of failure being in some ways the least of it. Without exception, judges are highly disturbed by an allegation of misconduct made against them. However, since their conduct is inevitably judged by their peers, the chance of real punitive action against them is minimal.

At best, an action of this sort might persuade a judge to remove himself from your case. However, even should this occur, the result will come at a high cost. Every judge who handles your file from that point on will be aware of what you have done, and it will be front and center as to every decision made effecting you and your child from that point on.

Again, this is an option that should be discussed with counsel. However, you should also keep in mind that your attorney, in all probability, will see your actions as a direct threat to his or her career. He or she will likely have to appear before the same judicial officers for years, and pay the costs of your actions long after you are gone. Judges are in many ways like most people, but are unique in having particularly long memories, as well as unchecked power.

If you live in a state in which judges are elected by the voters, there are other opportunities. If you find that there is a consensus that the judge in question is biased against those of the Christian faith, use the political system. There is no reason that the tactics utilized so successfully over the years by organizations opposed to traditional values cannot be used for good purposes. Consider options such as contacting elected officials, supporting alternative candidates, and protests. The failure of too many individuals of faith to take such actions is, in large measure, the reason for the situation we face today.

CHAPTER FOUR

DEALING WITH BIAS DURING THE TRIAL PROCESS

Of course, all such tactics have a limited upside. The truth is, if the system is sufficiently rotten, you will end up facing a hostile judge and an adverse guardian ad litem. Still worse, it is highly probable that, until the trial is over, you will not know the extent of the prejudice you face. This is because lawyers, above all things, learn early how to keep their mouths shut when necessary.

This leads to another important question. What can I do to increase my chance of winning in the face of such long odds? Actually, the answer is "More than you might think."

I say this because of certain impressions I have of judges, and of those who aspire to be judges (the majority of Guardians). At some point in the process, these individuals tend to become somewhat insular in their thinking.

This may be due to necessity. The job of family court judge is actually somewhat dangerous, leading many members of the judiciary to keep their heads low after hours. Partially as a result, they tend to spend their time with peers, trusted friends, and others who tend to think like themselves. These are not people who would be expected to challenge their preconceived notions and beliefs. As such, their misconceptions tend to be reinforced and harden over time.

Such is the nature of the uphill battle faced by a Christian in court before a judge who dislikes and distrusts Christians. His or her task is to identify the negative stereotypes which are consciously or unconsciously affecting the thinking of the trial judge.

This is not the sort of thing that has been studied. As such, it is necessary to essentially go on instinct and try to anticipate the mental blocks with which you might be dealing; that is, unless you get lucky and find some of these sentiments reduced to writing, which is highly unlikely. Anyway, here is my partial list. Feel free to add, delete, or edit based upon experience and instinct.

1. Christians are anti authoritarians who believe that they answer only to a supreme God, and do not respect governmental authority, particularly the courts.

2. Christians are intolerant and bigoted, and hate any and all of a disparate number of groups including homosexuals, feminists, Muslims, African Americans, or Hispanics.

3. Christians are a generally uneducated group.

4. Christians (males in particular) believe in an antiquated family structure dominated by the men, the women being barefoot, pregnant and submissive.

5. Christians, as a result, tolerate physical and psychological abuse of wives and children.

6. Christians see the world as evil, and isolate themselves and their children from outsiders who might challenge their belief system. They avoid diverse populations.

7. Christians (again particularly men) are a primary source group for terrorists.

8. Christians as a whole are a group with a unified set of core beliefs.

9. Christians hate and distrust science.

10. Christians as a group are an angry population.

At first glance, you probably find this list surprising and offensive. At second glance, there might be a subtle feeling of recognition, based upon residual memories of half watched TV shows. As we have discussed, there is little chance of finding out to what extent the person you are dealing in buys into this set of beliefs. However, one thing is certain. Taken together at face value, they are a vicious indictment with the capacity to close minds.

As with any set of unfair, stereotypical beliefs, the solution is to challenge and address misconceptions. Ironically, the same people who hold these poisonous ideas about Christians have spent years presuming to educate us as to how to correct our own thinking. While I will not agree that they were correct as to the need for same, I will concede that some of their methods, at least, are useful and effective.

Of course, there is a fine line between intelligently making the point that "I am not what you thought I was," and disavowing your faith. Finding the right side of that line is a near impossible game that you might well be forced to play.

At least the Bible does seem to establish some parameters relevant to the issue. The aforementioned letters of Paul, among other verses, establish the fact that it is entirely consistent with faith to respect state authority. Likewise, others sources, most prominently the life of Christ, make clear that it is also appropriate to challenge an authority which abuses its power. To determine what measures are called for in your particular case, you might consult your minister or attorney, or seek an answer in prayer.

That being said, here are some things that you should ALWAYS do, and NEVER do, when interacting with the presiding judge at trial, or the Guardian Ad Litem prior to or during trial.

1. ALWAYS show appropriate respect for the Judge, opposing counsel, and everyone else in the courtroom. You should dress

appropriately, which if you are a man means wearing a suit and tie. Stand when the Judge enters the courtroom, and also when you speak. Address individuals by their appropriate titles, and do not speak out of turn, unless it is for the purpose of objecting to a question (you will have your chance to speak later.)

This is important because it counters the impression that you have a hostile attitude towards the court, and its authority over your life and affairs. Doing these things properly might not do much to improve the result of your case, but I can tell you that failure to do so can cause a great deal of harm very quickly.

I once saw a Judge practically explode because my client kept looking at his wrist watch every few seconds. He told my client, at the top of his lungs, that if he were bored with the proceedings, he was welcome to leave. Judges, like everyone else, have their fair share of psychological and emotional issues.

2. There are catch phrases and buzzwords which should always be worked into your language when addressing the court. I realize that this sounds cynical. However, you can spend a great deal of time talking about your many friends, and never challenge a tacit assumption that you are bigoted and narrow minded because of your faith.

Unless it is patently untrue, you need to say that you want your child to "appreciate the diversity of our people and culture" and cite "tolerance and understanding" as a value you wish to pass on to your child. You may not use those exact words, but go with something closely approximating same. This rebuts any implication that you will segregate your child from society and teach him or her a narrow, dogmatic set of beliefs.

3. However, it is also appropriate and even necessary to openly acknowledge your faith. Despite all of the changes in our culture, the vast majority of Americans are of the Christian faith. While they may attend church far less often, or not at all, the fact remains that those are the

values upon which they were raised. Though many opinion shapers want to deny it, the Bible and the teachings of Christ are the touchstones upon which our culture, and by extension our law, was built.

The intent is not to deceive anyone about your beliefs, so be up front about them. Your purpose is merely to present them to the court in a way that others who do not share your faith can understand and appreciate. If you can do this successfully, you will have also shown that you are a caring and compassionate parent.

4. Because there is such a strong synergy between the legal code and the teachings of Christ, it is easy to explain most things in a secular manner. In most states, the question of custody is decided based upon the "best interests of the child." It is not necessary to reference Bible verses to explain why you desire to teach your child to be honest, respect property, etc. Remember that "being a good citizen" and "being a good Christian" are ultimately in many ways the same thing. Work in enough of the secular language to avoid alienating the fact finders.

5. Be aware that certain lawyers will see an advantage attempting to portray you as an irrational person or even a cultist. As such, you might find yourself being asked about your political and religious beliefs on the witness stand. You might be asked, for example, about your beliefs with regards to the end days or the tribulation, or your opinions with about homosexual marriage. Such questions should be objected to as irrelevant. If you have an attorney, he or she will take care of this.

6. There also seems to be a sentiment that Christians are predominantly gun owners, and that this can be a safety issue for a child. If you do in fact own a gun, anticipate that this might become an issue and be prepared.

This would mean having a proper license for the firearm. It might also mean having taken a gun safety course. Most importantly, it would mean having the gun under lock and key at all times so that there is no chance that the child could gain access to it. Possibly the quickest way to lose a custody action, or worse, your child, is to be careless with a firearm.

7. Avoid the urge to vent in public while the case is ongoing. This mean to avoid discussing the matter on social media sites such as Face book or Pintarest. A simple reference to the fact that there is a court date pending, and a request for prayers, can be found offensive by a Judge, particularly when his or her name or character is referenced.

I do not doubt the value and power of prayer, just suggesting that prayer requests be made in a relatively private and secure fashion.

8. If the other parent of your child is of another faith, restrain as much as possible from heated battles over access to the child for church and related activities. You can be sure that the child attends such functions when he or she is in your care, and it is fine to make civil requests of the other parent for additional or rescheduled time for this purpose. Avoid angry confrontation, including by way of e mail or text, which might become an issue at trial.

9. At all costs, do not lose your temper on the witness stand. This can be a difficult thing to do when the stakes are so extraordinarily high, and you are under attack. This is what your opposite number wants you to do. You win by keeping your cool.

10. Finally, win, lose or draw, keep in mind that however traumatic and hurtful the events of the day have been, your child has probably suffered through an even worse experience. Seek him or her out afterwards, and reassure her of your continuing love and presence in his life.

The Bible references cited earlier in the book are proof positive that such is your obligation as a parent and a believer in Christ.

CHAPTER FIVE

CHOOSING AN ATTORNEY

From day one of the process, you probably have a strong inclination as to whether you would want to hire an attorney. However, you might be a little less sure as to another question, "Can I be effectively represented by an attorney who is not of my faith?"

I believe that the answer to that question is yes. For an attorney to advocate in your best interests, and present your values and beliefs appropriately to the court, he or she does not necessarily have to be a devout Christian or a Christian at all. However, it is at least necessary that he or she at least respects and understands your beliefs.

It is easy enough to make this determination. At the initial interview, explain the importance of Christ to your day to day life, and to your parenting. Go into as much detail as you think necessary to explain how you feel you child should be raised, and why it is so important that you be given the opportunity to raise him or her in your faith. If the attorney yawns, rolls his eyes, or continually looks away, go elsewhere.

It goes without saying that a custody trial is one of the most important events in which you will participate in your life, right up there with marriage and the birth of the child. As such, I believe it is best to arrange initial consultations with at least three attorneys before making a decision, if there is time.

Each of them should have, at a minimum, these qualities:

1. He or she should have been in practice for at least three years, absent some evidence that the lawyer in question is a very quick learned. You do not want to a young lawyer cutting his teeth on a case of this importance.

2. He or she should practice regularly or exclusively in family court. In the majority of states, these cases are decided by a judge, which

means that the decisions are extremely relationship driven. There are a few movies about the lawyer who arrives in a strange town and saves his client from hanging, but reality it doesn't happen.

3. He or she should have a clean ethical record. This can easily be verified by searching his or her name on the state bar website. In fairness, it should be said that lawyer discipline in many states can be, to be kind, arbitrary and very political. However, there are certain offenses which are indicative of the character of the lawyer in question. For example, you do not want to hire anyone who misused client funds, has a history of neglecting files, or has committed perjury.

4. He or she should provide you with a written retainer agreement, which specifies the hourly rate at which you will be billed for services, and also what if any costs are payable by you. Do not pay an attorney any retainer until you have seen and executed such an agreement.

Also, keep in mind that everything is negotiable. There is no disgrace in asking the attorney if he would accept a smaller retainer, or reduce his hourly rate. Attorneys are subject to the effects of the bad economy just like everyone else, and most will be reluctant to let a potentially well paying client exit, especially if you have cash up front.

5. Lastly, if possible, try to negotiate a flat fee, which is the best option for saving money. This removes the possibility that a bill will be padded to compensate for a lower negotiated hourly rate, or a reduced retainer. If the attorney you wish to hire is not willing to agree to this, ask if he or she will instead agree to a fee "ceiling" or upper limit to the amount you will be billed. Such an agreement can save you thousands of dollars, and allow you to make financial plans for the future.

CONCLUSION

Always remember that, no matter how difficult the struggle, you are not alone:

When my enemies turn back, they shall fall and perish at your presence.

Psalm 9:3